D0178961

oxes

edators

...an

LL1(A)

raintree
a Capstone company — publishers for children

Raintree is an imprint of Capstone Global Library
Limited, a company incorporated in England and Wales
having its registered office at 7 Pilgrim Street, London,
EC4V 6LB – Registered company number: 6695582

www.raintreepublishers.co.uk
myorders@raintreepublishers.co.uk

Text © Capstone Global Library Limited 2015
First published in paperback in 2014
First published in paperback in 2015
The moral rights of the proprietor have been asserted.

Edited by Brynn Baker, Clare Lewis, and
     Helen Cox Cannons
Designed by Kyle Grenz and Tim Bond
Picture research by Tracy Cummins
Production by Helen McCreath
Originated by Capstone Global Library Limited
Printed and bound in China by Leo Paper Group

ISBN 978-1-406-28283-2 (hardback)
18 17 16 15 14
10 9 8 7 6 5 4 3 2 1

ISBN 978-1-406-28290-0 (paperback)
19 18 17 16 15
10 9 8 7 6 5 4 3 2 1

British Library Cataloguing in Publication Data
A full catalogue record for this book is available from
the British Library.

Acknowledgements
We would like to thank the following for permission to
reproduce photographs: Alamy: © age fotostock, 12, ©
blickwinkel, 18, 23b, © Picture Hooked/Malcolm Schuyl,
5, 23g, © Steven Mcgrath, 6, 23c, © tbkmedia.de, 15;
FLPA: Derek Middleton, 7 mouse, Imagebroker, 7 owl,
Michael Durham/Minden Pictures, 7 bat, Yva Momatiuk
& John Eastcott/Minden Pictures, 4, 10, 23e; Getty Im-
ages: malcolm park, 9, Philippe Henry, 17, Photographs
By Les Piccolo, 20; naturepl.com: Andrew Cooper,
14, 23d, Niall Benvie, 13, Stephen Dalton, 11, Terry
Whittaker/2020VISION, 19, 23a; Shutterstock: Michael
Wick, 16, 23f, ninikas, 21, Pim Leijen, 22, 23h, back
cover, Piotr Krzeslak, 7 hedgehog; Superstock: Nature
Picture Library, front cover

Every effort has been made to contact copyright holders
of material reproduced in this book. Any omissions will
be rectified in subsequent printings if notice is given to
the publisher.

Contents

What is a red fox?

A red fox is a small **mammal** with long legs and a bushy tail.

It has a long **snout** and pointed ears.

You might wonder why you rarely see red foxes during the day.

This is because they are **nocturnal**.

What does nocturnal mean?

Nocturnal animals are awake at night.

Animals that are nocturnal sleep during the day.

bat

owl

hedgehog

mouse

Many different animals are nocturnal.

Bats, owls, hedgehogs, and mice
are nocturnal.

Where do red foxes live?

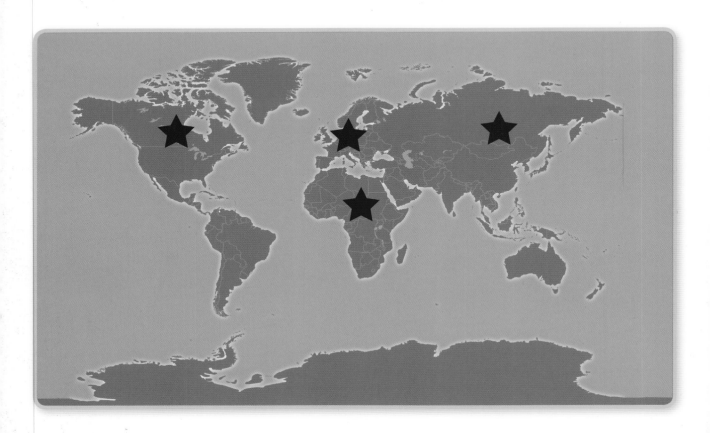

Red foxes live in North America, Europe, Asia, and Africa.

They can be found in forests, fields, mountains, and deserts.

Red foxes can even be found living near people.

They live in large gardens and near places where people throw away rubbish.

What do red foxes eat?

Red foxes are good hunters.

They eat small animals, such as rabbits, mice, and some birds.

Red foxes will also eat some plants and insects.

Foxes living near people will eat rubbish too.

Do red foxes have predators?

Red foxes are hunted by some large animals.

In some places, wolves, coyotes, and jackals hunt red foxes.

trap

Humans harm red foxes too.

Some people set traps to catch red foxes.

What are baby red foxes like?

Once a year, female red foxes give birth to a **litter** of babies.

Fox babies are called kits. Each litter has four to 10 kits.

Kits are born blind. They are covered with light grey fur.

After three months, the young foxes are ready to leave the **den** on their own.

What do red foxes do in winter?

Red foxes **mate** during winter.

They also hunt for animals, such as rabbits, pheasants, squirrels, and mice.

Red foxes stay warm in underground dens.

They wrap their fluffy tails around their bodies to stay warm.

How can you spot red foxes?

Look for red fox dens near rivers or streams.

The dens have large, oval-shaped openings.

Red foxes are most active at **dawn** or **dusk**.

You might spot one looking for food near a garden or park.

How can you help red foxes?

If you see a red fox, do not touch it.

Do not disturb red fox dens.

Do not use sprays or poisons to keep pests away.

Red foxes can eat these and get sick.

Red fox body map

ear

snout

tail

Picture glossary

 **dawn** time of day when the sun first rises

 **den** shelter for mammals

 **dusk** time of day when the sun sets

 **litter** number of baby animals born from one birth

 **mammal** warm-blooded animal that has a backbone, hair or fur, and gives birth to live babies that feed on milk from their mother

 **mate** when a male and female come together to breed

 **nocturnal** awake at night and asleep during the day

 **snout** part of an animal's head that projects forward and contains the nose and mouth

Find out more

Books

Red Foxes (Nocturnal Animals), J. Angelique Johnson, (Capstone Press, 2011)

Foxes (Exploring the World of), Tracy C. Read (Firefly Books Ltd, 2010)

Websites

Discover more nocturnal animals at:
http://bbc.co.uk/nature/adaptations/Nocturnality

Learn more about red foxes at:
www.rspca.org.uk/allaboutanimals/wildlife/inthewild/foxes

Index